Home

Book

Reference Manual for Your Home

Home Book: reference manual for your home

©2019 Traditions Press, Inc., Lexington, SC US

Designed and illustrated by nancy s taylor

ISBN# 9781796971323

The Home of

Established

Address

Insert photos

Insert photos

Comments and interesting facts about
the purchase and location of home...

notes

Exterior of Home

photo

Exterior of Home

Design Style: _______________________________

Period: ___________________________________

Materials: _________________________________

____

____

Landscaping: _______________________________

____

____

____

Trees: _____________________________________

Shrubs: ____________________________________

Plans for Improvements: _____________________

____

____

____

Entrance/Foyer

photo

notes

notes

Entrance/Foyer

Design Style: _________________________________

Paint: _________________________________

Wall finishing: _________________________________

____

____

____

Flooring:_________________________________

Furnishings: _________________________________

____

____

____

____

Plans for Improvements: _________________________________

____

____

____

notes

notes

Living Room

photo

notes

Living Room

Design Style: ______________________________

Paint: ______________________________

Wall finishing: ______________________________

____

____

____

Flooring:______________________________

Furnishings: ______________________________

____

____

____

____

____

Plans for Improvements: ______________________________

____

____

____

notes

notes

Kitchen

photo

notes

Kitchen

Design Style: _______________________________

Paint: _______________________________

Wall finishings: _______________________________

____

____

____

Flooring: _______________________________

Furnishings: _______________________________

____

____

____

____

Plans for Improvements: _______________________________

____

____

____

Kitchen Appliances

Refrigerator

Model:_______________________________________

Date:____

Warranty:____________________________________

____

Repair Service: ______________________________

____

Stove

Model:_______________________________________

Date:____

Warranty:____________________________________

____

Repair Service: ______________________________

____

Oven

Model:_______________________________________

Date:____

Warranty:____________________________________

____

Repair Service: ______________________________

____

Kitchen Appliances

Refrigerator

Model:____

Date:____

Warranty:______________________________________

____

Repair Service: _________________________________

____

Stove

Model:____

Date:____

Warranty:______________________________________

____

Repair Service: _________________________________

____

Oven

Model:____

Date:____

Warranty:______________________________________

____

Repair Service: _________________________________

____

Kitchen Appliances

____

Model:___________________________________

Date:____________________________________

Warranty:________________________________

____

Repair Service: __________________________

____

____

Model:___________________________________

Date:____________________________________

Warranty:________________________________

____

Repair Service: __________________________

____

____

Model:___________________________________

Date:____________________________________

Warranty:________________________________

____

Repair Service: __________________________

____

notes

notes

notes

Dining Room

photo

notes

Dining Room

Design Style: _______________________________

Paint: ___________________________________

Wall finishings: _______________________________

____

____

____

Flooring:_______________________________

Furnishings: _______________________________

____

____

____

____

____

Plans for Improvements: _______________________

____

____

____

notes

Den/Casual Room

photo

notes

Den/Casual Room

Design Style: _______________________________

Paint: _______________________________

Wall finishing: _______________________________

____

____

Flooring: _______________________________

Furnishings: _______________________________

____

____

____

____

____

Plans for Improvements: _______________________________

____

____

____

notes

Bedrooms

photo

snapshots of bedroom 1

Bedroom 1

Design Style: _______________________________________

Paint: _______________________________________

Wall finishings: _______________________________________

____

____

____

Flooring: _______________________________________

Furnishings: _______________________________________

____

____

____

____

____

Plans for Improvements: _______________________________________

____

____

____

snapshots of bedroom 2

Bedroom 2

Design Style: _______________________________

Paint: _______________________________

Wall finishings: _______________________________

____

____

____

Flooring: _______________________________

Furnishings: _______________________________

____

____

____

____

____

Plans for Improvements: _______________________________

____

____

____

snapshots of bedroom 3

Bedroom 3

Design Style: ________________________________

Paint: ________________________________

Wall finishings: ________________________________

____

____

____

Furnishings: ________________________________

____

____

____

____

____

Plans for Improvements: ________________________________

____

____

snapshots of bedroom 4

Bedroom 4

Design Style: ___________________________

Paint: ___________________________

Wall finishings: ___________________________

____

____

____

Flooring: ___________________________

Furnishings: ___________________________

____

____

____

____

Plans for Improvements: ___________________________

____

____

____

notes

Bathrooms

photo

Bathroom 1

Design Style: _______________________________

Paint: _______________________________

Wall finishings: _______________________________

____

____

____

Flooring:_______________________________

Furnishings: _______________________________

____

____

____

____

Plans for Improvements: _______________________________

____

____

____

Bathroom 2

Design Style: _______________________________

Paint: _______________________________

Wall finishings: _______________________________

____

____

____

Flooring: _______________________________

Furnishings: _______________________________

____

____

____

____

____

Plans for Improvements: _______________________________

____

____

____

Bathroom 3

Design Style: _______________________________

Paint: _______________________________

Wall finishings: _______________________________

____

____

____

Flooring: _______________________________

Furnishings: _______________________________

____

____

____

____

Plans for Improvements: _______________________________

____

____

____

notes

Additional Rooms

photo

snapshot

Room _______________________

Design Style: _______________________

Paint: _______________________

Wall finishings: _______________________

____

____

____

Flooring:_______________________

Furnishings: _______________________

____

____

____

____

____

Plans for Improvements: _______________________

____

____

____

Important Possessions

photos, descriptions...

Important Possessions

photos, descriptions...

Important Possessions

photos, descriptions...

Important Possessions

photos, descriptions...

Important Contacts

Service	Contact	Phone/email
Plumbing		
AC/Heating		
Insurance Agent		
Waste disposal		
Fire Department		
Police